NEW YORK REVIEW

POETS

M000211403

J.H. PRYNNE was born in Kent in 1936 and Cambridge University; he worked there as a teacher and scholar in the Department of English and is currently a life fellow of Gonville and Caius College. He is also an Honorary Professor at the University of Sussex, and a Visiting Professor at Sun Yat-Sen University, People's Republic of China. He has published forty-one collections of poems during the period 1968–2015, all now reprinted in the third enlarged edition of his *Poems* (Bloodaxe Books, Hexham, 2015).

This volume, *The White Stones*, was composed in the earlier 1960s, at the same time as working with students in the study of English and European poetry of various classical traditions, and also assimilating the force of the New American Poetry of that period. A good reading knowledge of French and German and Italian kept open a complex historical perspective, and an extremely partial understanding of Chinese demonstrated the influence of Ezra Pound in a new cross-light.

Since these early times there have also been extended commentary-essays, on the Han Chinese lyric, on a painting by Willem de Kooning, on literary/linguistic topics, and three extended commentary-monographs: on a Shakespeare sonnet, on a poem by Wordsworth and another by George Herbert, on Wallace Stevens, and on a scroll-painting by the Chinese landscape painter Shen Zhou (1425–1509). The author has traveled quite widely, in the U.S.A. and further afield; his poems have been translated into French, German, Italian, Norwegian and Chinese, and a brief selection is being prepared in Mexican Spanish; there have also been a number of musical settings and workings. His collected prose writings (2 vols) are currently in preparation. Some website material is available, including a full online bibliography and various talks and lectures.

PETER GIZZI is the author of several poetry collections, including *Threshold Songs*, *The Outernationale*, and most recently, *In Defense of Nothing: Selected Poems, 1987–2011*. His honors include the Lavan Younger Poet Award from the Academy of American Poets, and artist grants from the Foundation for Contemporary Arts, the Howard Foundation, and the Guggenheim Foundation. He has served as the poetry editor for *The Nation* and as founding editor of *o·blēk: a journal of language arts*. In 2011 and again in 2015–16 he was the Judith E. Wilson Visiting Fellow in Poetry at Cambridge University. He teaches at the University of Massachusetts, Amherst.

J.H. Prynne

The White Stones

INTRODUCTION BY PETER GIZZI

NYRB/POETS

 NEW YORK REVIEW BOOKS   *New York*

THIS IS A NEW YORK REVIEW BOOK
PUBLISHED BY THE NEW YORK REVIEW OF BOOKS
435 Hudson Street, New York, NY 10014
www.nyrb.com

Library of Congress Cataloging-in-Publication Data
    Names: Prynne, J. H., 1936– author.
Title: The white stones / J. H. Prynne ; introduction by Peter Gizzi.
Description: New York City : New York Review Books, [2016] | © 1969 |
    Series: New York Review Books Poets
Identifiers: LCCN 2015038047 | ISBN 9781590179796 (softcover : acid-free
    paper)
Subjects: | BISAC: POETRY / English, Irish, Scottish, Welsh. | POETRY /
    General.
Classification: LCC PR6066.R9 A6 2016 | DDC 821/.914—dc23
LC record available at http://lccn.loc.gov/2015038047

ISBN 978-1-59017-979-6
Available as an electronic book; ISBN 978-1-59017-980-2

Cover and book design by Emily Singer

Printed in the United States of America on acid-free paper.
10 9 8 7 6 5 4 3 2 1

Contents

INTRODUCTION

VERY FEW books of poetry published in England in the twentieth century have the aura of J. H. Prynne's *The White Stones*. The essential beauty of Prynne's work is a quality of mind. I vividly remember reading it for the first time in 1986 and being struck by its gorgeous surface structure and energetic belief system: It is a bright element, even psychedelic at times. Hard to believe that such a book would need an introduction, a book that has been passed from poet to poet for decades. It has long been, and remains, a touchstone.

The poems of *The White Stones* were written between 1964 and 1968. This was a period of great activity for Prynne, a time of many and new correspondences with British and American poets, and the inaugurations of various journals, most notably the Cambridge-based *The English Intelligencer*, edited by the poets Andrew Crozier and Peter Riley. Prynne was a central contributor of poems, essays, and letters to *The English Intelligencer*, where the majority of the poems in *The White Stones* were first published. Thirty-six issues appeared between 1966 and 1968, serving as a laboratory for an extended group of poets purposefully creating an

English countertradition. A year before the publication of *The White Stones* in 1969, Prynne published *Kitchen Poems* and *Day Light Songs*, the latter included in this new volume, as is the 1969 essay/prose poem "A Note on Metal."

Now, almost fifty years on, there is a large body of discourse about Prynne's work, but as soon as one tries to pin down the original signal of these poems it gets slippery. They refuse to be categorized: If they're Marxist, they're also heterodox; if they're romantic, they're also analytic; if they're scientific, they're also magical. And while Prynne's method shares cardinal features with Charles Olson's projective verse, the romantic philosophical inflection is closer to William Wordsworth, Friedrich Hölderlin, and late Wallace Stevens. When I first encountered Prynne's work, I felt that there was a braiding, like a double helix, of the Pound/Olson tradition with the Romantic/Stevens tradition, of high romanticism with physical, investigative, transhistorical inquiry.

In the course of the '60s Prynne developed deep and important friendships with some of the New American Poets, most notably Olson and Edward Dorn. In fact, after a voluminous correspondence with Olson, Prynne was responsible for preparing and editing the holographic manuscript of Olson's *Maximus IV, V, VI*. No mean task. There is an edition of the Prynne/Olson letters forthcoming from the University of New Mexico Press, which will further illuminate this important correspondence between these two brilliant and original men.

For this reason, it is worth rehearsing the elegant system that Olson proposed for an emancipatory poetics in his now venerable but still deeply relevant essay "Projective Verse." As Olson had it:

...The two halves are:

the HEAD, by way of the EAR, to the SYLLABLE
the HEART, by way of the BREATH, to the LINE

Olson further elucidates: "I am dogmatic, that the head shows in the syllable. The dance of the intellect..." and goes on to say, "And the threshing floor for the dance? Is it anything but the LINE?" The line in *The White Stones* works both at the line break and in the clausal phrases that keep the machine humming and dancing from one idea to the next, one subject to the next, while constantly opening the horizon of meaning that each poem proposes. The work is full of necessary and productive restlessness in the service of discovery, you can feel the breath driving the poem. The contracted and sometimes crabbed grammar creates rhythm, but the percussive quality of the diction creates something very physical. The ending of the poem "Song in Sight of the World" is a clear example of the syncopation produced from the technique of line and comma working together to both further and interrupt meaning:

The light will do all this, to
love is the last resort, you
must know, I will tell
you, this, love, is
                    the world.

There is a feeling in this book that a language is coming to the speaker of the poem in the very act of composition—that is, in real time. For example, in "First Notes on Daylight" we find:

> Patience is truly my device, as we wait
> for the past to happen, which is to come into
> the open. As I expect it to, daily...

These poems are faceted like crystal to daylight, or as Prynne would have it: "The striations are part of the heart's / desire." In many of the poems, this massing of clauses and perspectives creates an effect whereby any given singularity of personhood is defined and perhaps generated by a multiplicity of larger structural forces. In the magisterial poem "The Glacial Question, Unsolved," the temporal structure is the geologic time and weather of the British Isles:

> The falling movement, the light cloud
> blowing in from the ice of Norfolk
> thrust. As the dew recedes from the grass
> towards noon the line of recession
> slips back. We know where the north
> is, the ice is an evening whiteness.
> We know this, we are what it leaves:
> the Pleistocene is our current sense, and
> what in sentiment we are, we
> are, the coast, a line or sequence, the
> cut back down, to the shore.

In "Thoughts on the Esterházy Court Uniform," one of the most romantically charged poems in this volume, we encounter an interiority, a private meditation on the costuming of the court in which Joseph Haydn composed; we feel the pressure of composition and aesthetics within a ritualized social structure:

I walk on up the hill, in the warm
sun and we do not return, the place is
entirely musical. No person can live there
& what is similar is the deeper resource, the
now hidden purpose. I refer directly to my
own need, since to advance in the now fresh &
sprouting world must take on some musical
sense. Literally, the grace & hesitation of
modal descent, the rhyme unbearable, the
coming down through the prepared delay and
once again we are there, beholding the
complete elation of our end.

A metamorphic language is at play in these poems, where the voice is more observational than sentimental: Naming is the prerogative for knowing. In Prynne's conception, both court systems and glaciers are players in a larger formation, they endure now in their afterlife as a lyric poem.

There is a utopian energy in *The White Stones* continually wheeling outward, which is why this work will never become a nostalgic object: It is constantly *happening.* Its readers will find binding narratives, science, economics, romantic love, history, prehistory organically deployed throughout the book's soundscape. To dramatize this multiplicity, to make it real and active on the page is one of the standing achievements of *The White Stones*, the ambition of a voice enunciating scale.

This book retains a deep glamour by means of its undeniable beauty and phenomenal architecture, its intellect, its vocabularies, and its singular way to song.

Peter Gizzi

The White Stones

(1969)

Airport Poem: Ethics of Survival

The century roar is a desert carrying
too much away; the plane skids off
with an easy hopeless departure.
        The music, that it should
        leave, is far down
        in the mind
just as if the years were part of the
same sound, prolonged into the latent
            action of the heart.
        That is more: there
        affection will shoot it up
        like a crazed pilot. The desert
is a social and undedicated expanse, since
what else there is counts as merest propaganda.
        The heart is a changed
        petromorph, making
        pressure a social
intelligence: essential news
or present fact
over the whole distance back
and further, away.
        Or could be thus, as water
        is the first social fluency
        in any desert: the cistern
comes later and is an inducement of false power.
Which makes the thinning sorrow of flight
the last disjunction, of the heart: that
        news is the person, and love
        the shape of his compulsion
           in the musical phrase,
           nearly but not

yet back, into
the remotest
past.
Of which the heart is capable and will journey
over any desert and through the air, making
the turn and stop undreamed of:
love is, always, the
flight back
to where
we are.

A Figure of Mercy, of Speech

On the hilt of fortune: so that he
asks the time and it's grey, with
almost solemn insistence. Yes it is, so
that perhaps only the smell of resin

> holds him to a single
> hopefulness. She knows
> that, there is an oblique
> incitement, between them.

The branches dissolve upwards, into slivers
of the horizon: for each, the fear of this, or too
far into the side. The rift that she loves
to play, as forward, the sound of his breathing kind.

> In the light, that each
> might, running from both
> in reach to the distance
> that is unspoken, in the eye

where love is, and the sound of water, euterpe
shall it be called. They will play over
the slip, making the flesh and nails on the
handsome fingers, to the action of the light,

> will play the open palm
> hoping to keep to it, the fearful
> exaction of love: in grey light
> and hope in columns, by the river side.

The Stranger, Instantly

The tie only: how I want so much
to allow for it, the wish to know
where, in that face
                            which is an absent
match, to the spirit.
            So that a restless time
            prevails; my spine arches
with the wish that's here
                            as itself a note a sign
                            of who they are.
And are, sitting in all the hours
of love I must translate, out
                            back to the place
            where I feel it, as a local thing
            and want now
            to allow for:
to manage between the hands and hope
of the voice, that's it, there must be
                            a voice here also, lent
                            to but not taken—
since even from the edge the resting
                            waiting inshore is
travel as knowing, the quick
            placement of love as
            trust: at the source.
And so here, it is the others I most
                            take to, like stones
                            in the mist, in
                            the voice.

Living in History

Walk by the shore, it is
a cool image, of water
        a bearing into certain
        distinctions, as
        the stretch, out there
the temple of which way
he goes; and cannot shake
        the haze, from
        a list of small
        flames.
                He wants
only the patient ebb, as
following the shore: that's
        not honest, but where
        his foot prints and
        marks his track
            in the fact of
            the evening
the path where he grabs at
motion, like a moist plant
        or the worth, of
        hearing the tide come in.
Walk on it, being a line, of rest
and distinction, a hope now lived up
        to, a coast in awkward
        singular desires
            thigh-bone of the
            world

On the Anvil

Finely, brush the
sound from your
eyes: it rests
in the hollow

as looking in
the shops at both
reflections, in
the glass

        how
to move and the
sun slanting over
the streets: shielded
from the market

in the public
domain, as
taking the pace
of movement

in the hollow
furnished with that
tacit gleam, the
cavernous heart

The Holy City

Come up to it, as you stand there
that the wind is quite warm on the sides
of the face. That it is so, felt
      as a matter of practice, or
      not to agree. And the span,
to walk over the rough grass—all of this
is that we do, quite within acceptance
      and not to press
      the warm alarm
      but a light
      surface, a day
      lifted from high
      thick roots, upwards.
Where we go is a loved side of the temple,
a place for repose, a concrete path.
There's no mystic moment involved: just
      that we are
      is how, each
      severally, we're
      carried into
the wind which makes no decision and is
a tide, not taken. I saw it
      and love is
      when, how &
      because we
      do: you
could call it Ierusalem or feel it
as you walk, even quite jauntily, over the grass.

How It's Done

Always who turns is more than
the same, being in desire the pivot
of what he would most want: or
           in point of fact, they say,
           driving through the
           early morning, to go to it.
And this is true, therefore, in such sense
as the light will allow. We take leave
of it, in the prospect of being allowed, on
           as the rocks are, the folds
           let into the saddle, cut down
           to any hope, acquired.
All the rage of the heart reaches this lifted
point, then: a fashion of spirit, a made thing.
For this there is no name but the event,
           of its leaving. There is no
           lattice, we don't sit by
           the traffic lights bathing
the soul in the links of time. The place
rises, as a point of change. There are
rocks and trees as part of it, none in
           forms of evidence. Within
           limits this arena is
           where each one is allowed
to be: the movement to be found, in the
distance is the sound that I too hope for,
here at the rock point, of the world.

If There Is a Stationmaster at Stamford S.D. Hardly So

A matter of certain
   essential oils
                volatile
in the prolonged evening
        nor would he allow
   as the light stemmed
      back
   boarded up in the face of
that the line ran swiftly
        and skimming the
      crests only
into the hills of Vietnam

        With so little water
   the land creates a curved &
      muted extension
      the whole power is
just that, fantasy of control
   the dispersion, in such
      level sky
   of each pulse the sliding
      fade-through of hills
      "a noble evasion of privacy"

   This is parkland for
watered souls, the final
      policeman's dream
     that the quanta of wish
and desire, too, can be marched

off to some goal so distant
		where in the hermitage
		of our last days the
	handcuffs would seem
			an entirely proper
		abstraction:
			the dry and
arid gentleness, to the eye
	with its own confidence
			in the deep wells
			of the spirit

All no more than
			a land in drift
	curled over and dry, but
		buried way under the ice
	and as spillway for these
			glacial waters the
	scented air
			runs easily into the
			night and while
the public hope is as
		always the
			darkened ward
		the icecap will
			never melt
		again why
		should it

In the Long Run, to be Stranded

Finally it's trade that the deep changes
work with, so that the lives are heavier,
less to be moved from or blunted. The city
is the language of transfer
        to the human account. Here
        the phrases shift, the years
        are an acquiescence.
This isn't a wild comment: there's no
good in the brittle effort, to snap the pace
into some more sudden glitter of light:
        hold to this city or the slightly pale
        walking, to a set rhythm of
        the very slight hopefulness. That
is less than patience, it's time or more clearly
the sequence of years; a thickening in the words
as the coins themselves wear thin and could
        almost balance on the quick
        ideal edge. The stirring is so
        slight, the talk so stunned, the
city warm in the air, it is a
too steady shift and life as
it's called is age and the merest impulse,
        called the city and the deep
        blunting damage of hope.
        That's where it is, now
as the place to be left and the last
change still in return: down there
in the snow, too, the loyal city of man.

The Western Gate

Too far up, into the sky, so that
the hills slip with the wash of
the quick brightness. What could the weather
shift, by those changes of place?
                Manganese on the brow;
                the rich ore, clouds over
                the stars, coming inshore—
all the power of our sentiment, what we
do feel, wanting the inclusion, the shade.
Watch any road as it lies on the
seam of the earth, with that partly
                turning & falling metaphysic:
                we believe it even despite
                the engineers. The power
is the wish to move, to recognise a
concealed flame in the evening
or dawn or whatever. The gleam
is history, desire for a night sky
                during the day too, since
                the stars circle the hills &
                our motives without reproach.
The formal circuit is inclusion. The line runs
inflected but the shapes are blue & shining.
It is the orbit, tides, the fluctual spread,
we shiver with reason and with love:
                the hills are omens, & the
                weather how long, with
                the stars, we can wait.
Or, it rains and the camber of the road
slips into it too—it's all there, as
the brickwork or hope for advice.

Write a letter, walk across the wet pavement,
        the lines are taut with
        strain, maybe they'll
        snap soon. The explosion
is for all of us and I dedicate the results
to the fish of the sea and the purity of
language: the truth is sadder but who
would ask me to hope only for that?

Lashed to the Mast

9th Nov 65:
                    Thus you have everything, at this
                    moment, that I could ever
                    command or (the quaint word)
                    dispose; rising now
                    in the east or wherever
                    damn well else
it's yours but the old
weather must be (must still
be watched, thunder
is a natural phenomenon
                    the entire sequence
                    is holy, inviting, no
                    sympathy: who should dare
                    let that out, towards
                    what there is
                    anyway
        love the set, tight, the life
        the land lie & fall, between
        also the teeth, love the
        forgetfulness of man which
        is our prime notion of praise
                    the whole need is a due thing
                    a light, I say this in
                    danger aboard our dauncing boat
                    hope is a stern purpose &
                    no play save the final lightness
the needful things are a sacral
convergence, the grove on

a hill we know too much of—
this with no name & place
is us / you, I, the whole other

image of man

Fri 13

no one thing
to say, leaving
nothing but
all that smell of
      the sea
      (private
& the gulls, squawking
in the knowledge
of time, of nothing
      at all, here
      on the rim.
Viz, the shelf out
as a pillar to fortune
      the shoals a
      quick draw
or longer, which is
a width to be gauged
      by the most
      specific &
      hopeful
      eye

Break It

And again it finishes, as we should
say it's over, some completeness numbs me
with the final touch
                      we are sealed, thus
and why it should be so, well, that's life
not well, you see you see or we
do, we touch that, and
                         it's the last time or
thing or some edge. Like cliffs, the de-
parture is overwhelming as a casual
thread, leading into this, that, the
gray darkness.
                Call it evening the days
are no shorter but ah how they do
foreclose, that the tide turns and
the wick burns and curls and all

the acrid wavering of language, so full
of convenient turns of extinction. Phrase
falls, we call it an ancient city, as
we look down from
                   the heights, hugging
the only mountain for many miles.
Blessed, as we leave: that we do, how
we do what there is these are
                   the one thing:
where are you   I drift into what it
should be or have you do you have, would
you. Would you. Life is a gay bargain.

How could I say, where you are among
the mountains of the city in their midst.
Turn to the east, the west, the torque
at the waist running round
                              the ribs, and
settling there. The end of that is a
sorry thing, how much more
beautiful is the city than
                              the abrupt cliffs, the
                              end, of that?

Against Hurt

Endowed with so much
suffering, they should be / and that
they are so—the pain in the head
        which applies to me
        and the clouds low over
        the horizon: soon it
        will be dark
We love the brief night, for its
quick passing, the relative ease as
we slide into comfort and
        the trees grow and
        grow. I can hear
        every smallest growth
the expanse is grinding with it,
out on the flats beyond, down by
the sodium street-lights, in the head:
pain, the hurt to these who are all
        companions. Serenity
        is their slender means.
        There is not much time
left. I love them all, severally and in
the largest honour that there is.
Now and with the least hurt, this
        is for you.

Moon Poem

The night is already quiet and I am
bound in the rise and fall: learning
to wish always for more. This is the
means, the extension to keep very steady
          so that the culmination
          will be silent too and flow
          with no trace of devoutness.
Since I must hold to the gradual in
this, as no revolution but a slow change
like the image of snow. The challenge is
not a moral excitement, but the expanse,
          the continuing patience
          dilating into forms so
          much more than compact.
I would probably not even choose to inhabit the
wish as delay: it really is dark and the knowledge
of the unseen is a warmth which spreads into
the level ceremony of diffusion. The quiet
          suggests that the act taken
          extends so much further, there
          is this insurgence of form:
we *are* more pliant than the mercantile notion
of choice will determine—we go in this way
on and on and the unceasing image of hope
is our place in the world. We live there and now
          at night I recognise the signs
          of this, the calm is a
          modesty about conduct in
the most ethical sense. We disperse into the ether
as waves, we slant down into a precluded notion

of choice which becomes the unlearned habit of
wish: where we live, as we more often are than
  we know. If we expand
  into this wide personal vacancy
  we could become the extent
of all the wishes that are now too far beyond
us. A community of wish, as the steppe
on which the extension would sprinkle out
the ethic density, the compact modern home.
  The consequence of this
  pastoral desire is prolonged
  as our condition, but
I know there is more than the mere wish to
wander at large, since the wish itself diffuses
beyond this and will never end: these are songs
in the night under no affliction, knowing that
  the wish is gift to the
  spirit, is where we may
  dwell as we would
go over and over within the life of the heart
and the grace which is open to both east and west.
These are psalms for the harp and the shining
stone: the negligence and still passion of night.

Love in the Air

We are easily disloyal, again, and the light
touch is so quickly for us, it does permit
what each one would give in the royal
use of that term. Given, settled and
broken, under the day's sun: that's the pur-
pose of the gleam from my eyes, cloud from
the base of the spine. Whose silent
watching was all spent, all foregone—
the silver and wastage could have told you
and allowed the touch to pass. Over the
brow, over the lifting feature of how
slant in the night.
                              That's how we
are disloyal, without constancy to the little
play and hurt in the soul. Being less than
strict in our gaze; the day flickers and
thins and contracts, oh yes and thus does
get smaller, and smaller: the northern
winter is an age for us and the owl of
my right hand is ready for flight. I have
already seen its beating search in the sky,
hateful, I will not look. By our lights
we stand to the sudden pleasure of how
the colour is skimmed to the world, and our
life does lie as a fallen and slanted thing.

If he gives, the even tenor of his open
hands, this is display, the way and through
to a life of soft invasion. Is constancy
such a disloyal thing. With the hurt wish
torn by sentiment and how very gross our

threshold for pain has become. And the
green tufted sight that we pass, to and
from, trees or the grass and so much, still
permitted by how much we ask.

I ask

       for all of it, being
       ready to break
       every constant thing.
       We are bound and
       we break, we let loose
       what we nakedly hold

           thus, he turns
           she watches, the
           hills slip, time
           changes hands.

I ask for it all, and the press is the sea
running back up all the conduits, each
door fronting on to the street. What you can
afford is *nothing*: the sediment on which we stand
was *too much*, and unasked for. Who is the
light linked to the forearm, in which play
and raised, up off the ground. I carry you for-
ward, the motion is not constant but may
in this once have been so, loyalty is
regret spread into time, the hurt of how
       steadily and where
       it goes. She feels
       the glimpse over
       the skin. She is
       honest: she loves

           the steady
           fear. The
           durable fire.

And what you own, in this erotic furtherance,
is nothing to do with response or that
times do change: the matter is not to go
across, ever, making the royal deceit de nos jours.
As each one slips and descends, you could call
it coming down to the streets and the seedy
broken outskirts
                              of the town.

Bronze : Fish

We are at the edge of all that and
can reach back to another
matter, only it's not back but
down rather, or in some involved
sense of further off. The virtues
of prudence, the rich arable soil:
but why should ever the whole
mercantile harvest run to form
again? The social cohesion
of towns is our newer ligature,
and the binding, you must see, is
the rule for connection, where we
are licensed to expect. That's
the human city, & we are
now at the edge of it. Which way
are we facing. Burn the great sphere:
count them, days of the week.

For a Quiet Day

There are some men that focus
on the true intentness, as I know
and wouldn't argue with: it is
violent, the harp—I will not do it
       though, and the time is
       so gentle, in the shadow
       that any youth might
       sleep. But I will
not do it, with the gilded harp
and of all things, its pedals, for
the nice touch. As the curves too
are sometimes gentle, where we shall be
       in the succession of
       light, hope, the
       evening
distracts: and it is always too
fine, too hopeless and will not let
the gentle course—by the chance
rise of a voice.
       And if the intentness
       is the more true, then
       I want the gentler
       course, where
the evening is more of what we are:
or the day as well—moist, casual,
broken by inflictions of touch. This
is the resting-place, out in the street.
       That we are so, and
       for the other thing
       I will not do it, will
       not; this is a quiet day.

Just So

How long they ask, we ask, it
is the question. So much time to
travel or stop and yet the heart
is so slow & reluctant
            leave it, that's one
            way—there, on the
            ground: I love you
so, here but how long again, the
history of what we allow, are per-
mitted to have. A life for this
branch, dividing in the headlights
            waiting, the beam in
            prism, play or the sound
            in a great arc for the
world, it is an open fire, a hearth
stone for the condition of trust.
Don't ever wait for that. Twist it
out, in ply and then run, for
            the door: we must
            have the divine sense,
            of entrance. The way
in as what it is, not which then, or
how long as the question. Such things
are, the world is that fire, it burns
along all the horizons. It is
            the heart, where we
            are. I love you, so
            much. As this, as
this, which is for even more than I
could tell. The night flickers and
the day comes; has, will come. That's

the question, the mark strapped to
                   the hands; not the
                   eyes. Trust them, the
                   fire of the mind, lust
of the pure citizen, on every path
of the earth. The soil, tarmac, grass,
remorse, the sea, love in the air
we breathe. Fire on the hearth. The life
                   in what I now have
                   and listen to, just so
                   long, as we are.

Mouth Open

To set a name to it, hold them
down and ask merely
are they shouting, with both feet
planted and leaning towards me

> the note forming no con-
> sequence, they gulp the
> landscape before them

Alert, to the name of an occasion
which is theirs as I take
it from them, the offered gift
met by the purest sound

> I cannot hold this
> it is a name: shouting
> or leaning, on the single

earth which is below them, each one

From End to End

Length is now quite another thing; that is,
waiting or coming right up slap into the sun,
spreading into the land to cross, the smell of
diesel oil on the road. The friends there are,
as if residing in what instantly goes with it,
as if longer than the infinite desire, longer
and across into some other thing. Keeping
the line, running back up into the mountains,
denied. And so, in the actual moment dis-
honest, actually refusing the breakage, and
your instinct for the whole purpose
                        again shows
            how gently it is all broken
            and how lightly, as you
                        would say, to come in.
All the milky quartz of that sky, pink and
retained, into the sun. See such a thing climb
out of the haze, making the bridge straight
down into the face—which way, this way,
length beyond this, crossed. The dawn thing
suddenly isn't tenuous, and the reach back to
the strand is now some odd kind of debris:
                        how strange to
            say this, which abandons of
            course all the joy of not
                        quite going, so far.
I would not have recognised it if the sun
hadn't unexpectedly snapped the usual ride,
and with you a real ironist, your length
run off out into some other place. Not the
mountains, nothing to do with the sacred child.

The continued quality I know is turned down,
pointed into the earth: love is a tremor, in
this respect, this for the world without length.
Desire is the turn to a virtue, of extent
                    without length. How
         I feel is still along this path,
         down the cancelled line and
                    even in the dawn
as almost a last evening, coming back the
day before. Where they all live, and to say
such a thing is as you say it, promptly no
clouds but the sun. How else, in the face
of so much prudence, as the total staff of life;
as the friends, glittering (who would ever have
been ready for that? The sun, the red
                    shift; your hair
         is at the moment copper, a
         bronze mark, and the absurd
                    gift is just some
allowance, a generous move. How would that
ever have been so, the length taken down and
my nervous rental displayed. Not just holding
or drawing the part. You are too ready, since I
know you still want what we've now lost, into
the sun. Without either, the mark of our light
and the shade as you walk without touching
the ground. Lost it, by our joint throw,
and the pleasure, the breakage is no longer, no
more length in which we quickly say
good-bye, each to each at the meridian. As now
each to each good-bye I love you so.

The Wound, Day and Night

Age by default: in some way this must
be solved. The covenants that bind
into the rock, each to the other
are for this, for the argon dating
      by song as echo of the world.
      O it runs sweetly by, and prints over
      the heart; I am supremely happy,
the whole order set in this, the
proper guise, of a song. You can hear
the strains from so far off: withdrawn
      from every haunted place
      in its graveness, the responsive
      shift into the millions of years.
I am born back there, the plaintive chanting
under the Atlantic and the unison of forms.
It *may* all flow again if we suppress the
      breaks, as I long to do,
      at the far end of that distance
      and tidings of the land;
if we dissolve the bars to it and let run
the hopes, that preserve the holy fruit on the tree,
casting the moist honey, curing the poppy of sleep.
      "And in variety of aspects
      the sum remains the same,
      one family"—
that it be too much with us, again as
beyond that enfeebled history: that we be
born at long last into the image   of love

The Glacial Question, Unsolved

In the matter of ice, the invasions
were partial, so that the frost
was a beautiful head
                  the sky cloudy
and the day packed into the crystal
as the thrust slowed and we come to
a stand, along the coast of Norfolk.
That is a relative point, and since
the relation was part to part, the
gliding was cursive; a retreat, followed
by advance, right to north London. The
moraine runs axial to the Finchley Road
including hippopotamus, which isn't a
joke any more than the present fringe
of intellectual habit. They did live as
the evidence is ready, for the successive
drift.
        Hunstanton to Wells is the clear
margin, from which hills rise into
the "interior"; the stages broken through
by the lobe bent south-west into the Wash
and that sudden warmth which took
birch trees up into Scotland. As
the 50° isotherm retreats there is
that secular weather laid down in pollen
and the separable advances on Cromer (easterly)
and on Gipping (mostly to the south).
The striations are part of the heart's
desire, the parkland of what is coast
inwards from which, rather than the reverse.
And as the caps melted, the eustatic rise

in the sea-level curls round the clay, the
basal rise, what we hope to call "land".

And the curving spine of the cretaceous
ridge, masked as it is by the drift, is
wedged up to the thrust: the ice fronting
the earlier marine, so that the sentiment
of "cliffs" is the weathered stump of a feeling
into the worst climate of all.
                              Or if that's
too violent, then it's the closest balance that
holds the tilt: land/sea to icecap from
parkland, not more than 2°–3° F. The
oscillation must have been so delicate, almost
each contour on the rock spine is a weather
limit
          the ice smoothing the humps off,
filling the hollows with sandy clay
as the litter of "surface". As the roads
run dripping across this, the rhythm
is the declension of history, the facts
in succession, they *are* succession, and
the limits are not time but ridges
and thermal delays, plus or minus whatever
carbon dates we have.
                          We are rocked
in this hollow, in the ladle by which
the sky, less cloudy now, rests on our
foreheads. Our climate is maritime, and
"it is questionable whether there has yet been
sufficient change in the marine faunas
to justify a claim that
                          the Pleistocene Epoch itself
has come to an end." We live in that

question, it is a condition of fact: as we
move it adjusts the horizon: belts of forest,
the Chilterns, up into the Wolds of Yorkshire.
The falling movement, the light cloud
blowing in from the ice of Norfolk
thrust. As the dew recedes from the grass
towards noon the line of recession
slips back. We know where the north
is, the ice is an evening whiteness.
We know this, we are what it leaves:
the Pleistocene is our current sense, and
what in sentiment we are, we
are, the coast, a line or sequence, the
cut back down, to the shore.

REFERENCES

Ordnance Survey Limestone Map, Sheets 1 and 2 (1955 edition), with Explanatory Text (1957)

K. W. Butzer, *Environment and Archaeology; An Introduction to Pleistocene Geography* (London, 1965), especially chapters 18, 21, 22, 28

W. B. R. King, "The Pleistocene Epoch in England," *Quart. Journ. Geol. Soc.*, CXI (1955), 187–208

R. P. Suggate and R. G. West, "On the Extent of the Last Glaciation in Eastern England," *Proc. Roy. Soc.* B, 150 (1959), 263–283

G. Manley, "The Range of Variation of the British Climate," *Geogr. Journ.*, CXVII (1951), 43–65

R. G. West and J. J. Donner, "The Glaciations of East Anglia and the East Midlands: a differentiation based on stone-orientation measurements of the tills," *Quart. Journ. Geol. Soc.*, CXII (1956), 69–87

Charm Against Too Many Apples

Still there is much to be done, on the
way into the city, and the sky as yet
only partly written over; we take all
our time and the road is lined with apple trees.
That's where we go, then, and if this sounds
too obviously prolonged, remember that
the ice was our prime matter. Flame is only
just invisible in sunlight

                          and the smoke goes
wavering into the atmosphere with all the
uncertainty of numbers. And so we can't
continue with things like this, we can't simply
go on. In this way through the forest, we
lose too much and too quickly: we have
too much to lose. How can anyone hope,
to accomplish what he wants so much not
finally to part with. We even pick up
the fallen fruit on the road

                         frightened by the
layout of so much *fallen,* the chances we know
strewn on the warm gravel. Knowing that
warmth is not a permanence, ah we count
on what is still to be done and the keen
little joys of leaves & fruit still hanging up
on their trees.

                  Whereas I wish that it would
all drop, or hang in some other way suspended;
that we should not be so bribed, by incom-
pletion. The ransom is never worth it and

we never get it anyway. No one can eat so
many apples, or remember so much ice. I

wish instead that the whole federate agency
would turn out into and across the land.
With any circling motion it could be so easily
for them, theirs as a form of knowledge, and we
would rest in it: the knowledge that *nothing
remains to be done*. What we bring off is
ours by a slip of excitement: the sky is our eternal
city and the whole beautiful & luminous trance
of it is the smoke spreading
                              across into the upper air.

First Notes on Daylight

Patience is truly my device, as we wait
for the past to happen, which is to come into
the open. As I expect it to, daily & the ques-
tion is really what *size* we're in, how much of
it is the measure, at one time. Patience is
the sum of my inertia, by which the base-line
lays itself out to the touch
   like the flower in
   heaven, each pebble
   graded in ochre. How
to extend, anyway to decline the rhetoric
of *occasion*, by which the sequence back
from some end is clearly predictive. We
owe that in theory to the history of person
as an entire condition of landscape—*that*
kind of extension, for a start. The open
fields we cross, we carry ourselves by ritual
observance, even sleeping in the library.
   The laggard, that is,
   whose patience
   is the protective
   shield, of the true
   limit to *size*.
"The ceremonial use of the things described",
the *činar* trees or the white-metal mirror, forms
of patience, oh yes, and each time I even
move, the strophic muscular pattern is *use*, in
no other sense. The common world, how far we
go, the practical limits of daylight. And as I
even think of the base-line the vibration is

strong, the whole sequence of person as his
own history is no *more* than ceremonial,
   the concentration
   of intersect: dis-
   covery back to
   the way over, the
entire crossing an open fabric, which we wear
stand on or carry in the hand. That this could
really be so & of use is my present politics,
burning like smoke, before the setting of fire.

Frost and Snow, Falling

That is, a quality of man and his becoming,
beautiful, or the decoration of some light and
fixed decision, no less fluent than the river
which guards its name. The preservative
of advice, keeping to some kind of order,
within the divine family of ends. The snow
level is where it fell and the limit thus
of a long cadence, the steppe whitening
in the distance and the winter climate.
The fall of snow, as of man in the ice block
and its great cracking roar, is a courtesy;
we don't require the black spiral, being gentle
and of our own kind. We run deeper, cancel
the flood, take to the road or what was before
known as champaign. We stand off the shore
even when turning to our best and most serious
portions of time. I judge that, as a snow level
but equally in seasonal pasture, pleasure or
as the rival comes, with clay on his shoes.
How far have you come and how long was your
journey? Such persons are hungry; the rival
ventures his life in deep water, the reddish gold
glints in the shadows of our lustful solitude.

So that when the snow falls again the earth
becomes lighter and lighter. The surface con-
spires with us, we are its first-born. Even
in this modern age we leave tracks, as we
go. And as we go, walk, stride or climb
out of it, we leave that behind, our own
level contemplation of the world. The monk

Dicuil records that at the summer solstice
in Iceland a man could see right through the
night, as of course he could. That too is a
quality, some generous lightness which we
give to the rival when he comes in. The tracks
are beaten off, all the other things underground.

On 9th May 1247 they set out on the return
journey. "We travelled throughout the winter, often
sleeping in the desert on the snow except when
we were able to clear a place with our feet.
When there were no trees but only open country
we found ourselves many a time completely
covered with snow driven by the wind." That
sounds to me a rare privilege, watching
the descent down over the rim. Each man
has his own corner, that question which
he turns. It's his nature, the quality he
extends into the world, just as his stature is
his "royal dignity". And yet Gregory did not
believe in the pilgrimage of place: Jerusalem,
he says, is too full of rapine and lust to be
a direction of the spirit. The rest is some kind
of flame, the pilgrim is again quality, and
his extension is the way he goes across the crust
that will bear him. The wanderer with his
thick staff: who cares whether he's an illiterate
scrounger—he is our only rival. Without this
the divine family is a simple mockery, the
whole pleistocene exchange will come to
melt like the snow, driven into the ground.

For This, For This

The next stave we come to is the mansion
or house, wondering about the roof and the
set, as it were, back into the silence which
is the social division, split into quietness.
Why are we so tensed as we prepare to make
some side step, into the house and thus, you
would say, out of the world. Off the planet
even, while the amber glow of Mercury shines
from the flashing shield? Oh no it's not this,
any more than we deny the sound its direction,
choosing to "hear" the splinter and splash
of some ordinary thing.

> I will not listen, or claim
> to, that ignoble worship of
> the wrong road. They are
>   too clean, always, they
>   fall in part to part, this knife
>   will go straight into
>   the fire if that's the heart.

And þerto when þou seest þat alle soche werkes in þeire
use mow be boþe good & iuel, I preie þee leue hem boþe,
for þat is þe most ese for þee for to doo if þou wilt
be meek.

> Watch the colour run up the blade; watch the
> house held off, we live so much in this way.
> How does he know when to "speak his mind"
> and come back in through some pattern of

45

misery? Buying his way in through this price
making the doorway, and now even current coin
is frozen in the banks; some weird puritan
stringency that believes cold to be bracing.

　　　All the quick motions
　　　as we nip upstairs, turn
　　　to steps we take: leading
　　　　　to the moral exits
　　which we see enjoined. Some idea of
　　　　　　completeness; protection
　　　is wretched and what we pay for.

And leue þe corious beholdyng & seching in þi wittes to
loke wheþer is betir.

Yet some soft stirring to speak is in the air,
the casual motion flirts with us. We are
less sombre now, slipping out at the door
and into some silent affair through which
we hear everything. All of that, without
name, not with regret, as a musical turn.
The importance is complete, the sequence
is urban, needful; she comes like some
obvious choice, picking her way. I see
this, you see the world in her wide sails,

　　　the knife is not playful
　　　or an agent of just
　　　device. It comes from
　　　　　the kitchen, I'm not
　　going to tell you that; you know
　　　　　how outside the door too
　　　we are ready in one.

Bot do þou þus: sette þe tone on þe to honde and þe toþer on þe toþer, and chese þee a þing þe whiche is hid bitwix hem, þe whiche þing when it is had, ȝeueþ þee leue, in fredom of spirite, to beginne and to seese in holding any of þe oþer at þin owne ful list, wiþouten any blame.

In Cimmerian Darkness

When the faint star does take
    us into the deeper parts
    of the night there *is*
       that sudden dip
and we swing across into
        some other version of this
    present age, where any curving
    trust is set into
the nature of man, the green raw and fabulous
love of it, where every star that shines,
    as he said, exists
in love, the *brother*
       dipping into the equal limit,
    help as the ready art, condition of the
    normal
       since no more simple
presence will fade, as the dawn does, over
water, the colonies of feeling like stacks
       of banknotes waiting to be counted.
Anyone waits, the brother is a section of
    the waiting art, whereby and
    through which agency the whole
cosmic vibrations disport their limbs, their
       hopes, the distant repose.
    We dip into the ready world
       which waits for us: the
name of it is our brother and we must pro-
       tect what we want of it,
    as we need more than I personally
    can ever admit. Or now do so
admit, the title to this going into the sky

is the trust of the lighted brother in the
first sense, the *standard*.
Stand there, I implore you, the trust *is* an agency
of surrender, I give it all up, the star
is yielded. No part of this dipping
coil shall be withheld; no
light further than the figure of some complete
fortune, making and made weak
by affection and the promise of it.
Led to the star, trusting to rotten planks,
the equal limit, we must have it, I ask only
in sequence, in this parity of
art ready with its own motion. It swings out
and we are quickly cruel, the brother reforms
his wish to roam the streets, he
should refuse as much as he can.
Nor is the divine in any sense
full, the vacancy stretches away
to the standard out on the plain; the cups
of our radio telescopes stand openly
braced to catch the recoil. Focus, the
hearth is again warm, again the human patch
waits, glows in the slight wind.
And we *are* ready for this, the array *is* there in
the figure we name brother, the
fortune we wish for, devoutly, as the dip
turns us to the face we have
so long ignored; so fervently refused.

Song in Sight of the World

In sight of the world they are
heavy with this, the sea
thrown up, the shore and all
the lamps out on the road—
       but where are they, will
       they go to: why do
       not love and instruction
       come swiftly to the places
where they stand? Who are the muses
in this windblown instalment—as
if there is much uncertainty
about that. We are a land
       hammered by restraint, into
       a too cycladic past. It is
       the battle of Maldon binds
       our feet: we tread
only with that weight & the empire
of love, in the mist. The name of this
land, unknown, is that. Heavy with sweat
we long for the green hills, pleasant with
       waters running to the sea
       but no greater love. The politics
       of this will bear inspection. They are
       the loss of our each motion, to history.
Which is where the several lost stand
at their various distance from the shore
on gneiss or the bones of a chemical plan
for the world's end. This is it, Thule,
       the glyptic note that we carry
       with every unacted desire felt
       in the continent of Europe. Lot's

           wife, the foreshore of the world.
And the weight? Still with us, the hold
is a knowing one. The night is beautiful
with stars: we do not consider the end
which is a myth so powerful, as to throw
           flames down every railway line
           from London to the furthest tip
           cape and foreland left by the axe.
           Apollo it is that I love, that
shall be swallowed by the great wolf and be
reborn as a butterfly in the hair of a goddess.
We are poor in this, but I love
and will persist in it, the equity
           of longing. The same is not true
           but desired: I desire it and shall
           encircle the need with bands of iron,
           this is the wedge of my great hope.
All the shores are a single peak. All the
sea a great road, the shore a land in
the mist. The tears of the world are spread
over it, and into the night you can hear
           how the trees burn with foreknowledge.
           As before, I am the great lover
           and do honour to Don Juan, & sharpen
           his knife on the flat of my foot.
The forest, of stars. The roads, some grey
people walking towards the restaurant.
The headlights, as a lantern; now they are
in the restaurant. See, we shall eat them.
           The light will do all this, to
           love is the last resort, you
           must know, I will tell
           you, this, love, is
                       the world.

Quality in that Case as Pressure

Presence in this condition is quality
which can be transformed & is subject
even to paroxysm—but it is not
lapse: that is the chief point. As I
move with my weight there is collusion,
with the sight of how we would rise
or fall or on the level. How *much* we
see is how far we desire change, which
is transformation from the ridge and fore-
land *inverted*—with all the clouds
over the shore.

> The sun lies on the
> matching of the ridge, &
> passing is what you
> cannot have, it is
> > the force, where
> > else to see
> > how in, this
> > is, the oblique

turned into a great torque which is
pleasure as a name for each part:
no nearer than

> the ridge, or side
> slope end time so
> much but not *how*

much. My own satisfaction in this
mild weather is violent; I am moved
by the *condition* of knowledge, as the
dispersion of form. Even, tenuous, gorged
in the transgressions of folding

> the orogeny of passion the

invasion of ancient
seas
    the neutral
    condition of
    that
the heart/heartland, prize
of the person who can be
seen to stumble & who falls with joy, unhurt.
Or who hurries, on some pavement, the
sublate crystal locked for each step.
They aim their faces but also bear them
and have cloth next to most of their skin.
    They are the children of proof.
    The proof is a *feature*, how the
    spine is set. The invasion
        of fluid, where the
        action of money
        is at least tem-
        porarily displaced.
By seepage or transgression, the mineral salts
"found their way" into the Zechstein Sea. The
reciprocation of fault and inversion,
poverty the condition, of which I am so clearly
guilty I can touch the pleasure involved.

For such guilt is the agency of ethical fact:
we feel shame at the mild weather too and
when the National Plan settles comfortably
like a Grail in some sculpted precinct
        I am transported
        with angelic
        nonchalance.
The quantities of demand are the measure
of want—of lack or even (as we are told)

sheer grinding starvation. *How much* to
eat is the city in ethical frenzy
>   the allowances set against
>   tax the deductions in respect
>   of unearned income
the wholly sensuous & mercantile matter
of *count*. As I move through the bright
bones of their hands & faces
>   shattered by the exact
>   brimming of love &
>   pleasure, the force
>>   is a condition
>>   released in the
>>   presence
>>   *that*
this is the chosen remnant, of a plan
now turned on its axis, east-west into the
wind. I am bound to it, by an aggressive
>   honour, and
in this the peace of the city does now reside.

Oil

In the year; intact in the cycle of days
   passing over him like the damp air
     he is back on the first level,
   some floating completeness
           has assailed him. He
is perfect. In the sight of his eye the
   wind dripping with rain
has come so far, round over the crests
       and fields, the cornea moist the
       lymph draining and curled
down to rest. This level sequence of history
   is his total and our total
     also, is
the certain angular sustenance
   of the world. So I walk over the
top of the steady and beating level of his
   eye; he has so much to bestow, he is
    generous. What he has is our
shout, the sound of the pathway, going down into
   the breathing touch of the air, the rain
   which soaks into our clothes. At last
    we are wet,
   wet through with what we have
in his eye, in our time, in the ribs in-
    flated with it, the
        last few days of the year

Shadow Songs

1

The glorious dead, walking
barefoot on the earth.
Treat them with all you
have: on the black marble
and let Nightingale come
down from the hills.
Only the procession is halted
as this spills down into
the current of the river:
their glorious death, if
such on earth were found.

2

And if the dead know this,
coming down into the dark, why should
they be stopped? We are too gentle
for the blind to see or be heard.
All the force of the spirit lies open
in the day, praise in the clock face
or age: the years, with their most
lovely harm. Leading the gentle
out into the wilds, you know they
are children, the blind ones, and
the dead know this, too.

Concerning Quality, Again

So that I could mark it; the continuance of
quality could in some way be that, the time
of accord. For us, as beneath the falling water
      we draw breath,
      look at the sky.
Talking to the man hitching a lift back
from the hospital, I was incautious in sympathy:
will she be back soon I was wishing to
encourage his will to suppose. I can hardly
expect her back he said and the water
fell again, there was this sheet, as the time
      lag yawned, and quality
      became the name you have,
like some anthem to the absent forces of nature.
Ethnic loyalty, breathe as you like we in fact
draw it out differently, our breath is gas
in the mind. That awful image of choking.

We *have* no mark for our dependence, I would
not want to add a little red spot to the wrist of
the man in the newsreel, the car passing the lights.
I draw blood whenever I open my stupid mouth,
      and the mark is on *my* hand, I
      can hardly even feel the brass wire
      nailed down into the head.
Paranoid, like the influencing machines; but who
they are, while their needs shine out like flares,
that quality *is* their presence outward to the night
sky: they do ask for that casual aid. The re-
cognition is accident, is an intolerable fall like
water. We whizz on towards the blatant home

and the armies of open practice. His affairs are
electric; they cancel the quality of the air;
      the names are a blankness as
      there are no marks but the wounds.

Even the accord, the current back (for him as for
me outward) has an electric tangent. He could
have flown off just there as he was. Simply
moved sideways, in his sitting posture, across the
next hedge and into a field I know but could
not recognise. The mark is Abel's price, the
breath is blood in the ears as I even dare to think
of those instruments. The sky is out there with
the quality of its pathic glow, there is a bright
thread of colour across the dashboard; the accord
      is that cheap and we live
      with sounds in the ear
      which we shall never know.

On the Matter of Thermal Packing

In the days of time now what I have
is the meltwater constantly round my feet
and ankles. There the ice is glory to the
past and the eloquence, the gentility of
the world's being; I have known this
as a competence for so long that the
start is buried in light

       usual as the warm grass and shrubbery
       which should have been ancestral
       or still but was, then, bound like crystal
       into the last war. There was a low
       drywall, formal steps

down I now see to the frozen water, with
whitened streaks and bands in it;
the same which, in New England, caused
a total passion for skating, and how still
it all was

             the gentility of a shell, so
                fragile, so beautifully
           shallow in the past; I
                hardly remember
             the case hardened
                  but brittle

constant to the eighteenth century or the
strictly English localism of moral candour,
disposed in the copses of those fields
which bespoke easily that same vague lightness,
that any motion could be so much

borne over the
top, skimming
not knowing the flicker
that joins
I too

never knew who had lived there. It was then
a school of sorts, we were out of the bombs
I now do, I think, know that. But the flow
so eloquently stopped, walking by the Golden
Fleece and the bus time-table

("It is difficult
to say pre-
cisely what
constitutes
a habitable
country"—A
Theory of the Earth

the days a nuclear part
gently holding the skull or
head, the skin porous to the
eloquence of

where this was so far! so ice-encased like
resin that whiteness seemed no more, than
cloudy at that time. The water-pattern is
highly asymmetric, bonding hardly as proof
against wealth, stability, the much-loved ice.

Which I did love, if
light in the field
was frozen
by wire

                        ploughed up, I
                did not know, that
                        was the gentle
                                reach of ignorance
                the waves, the
                        ice

the forms frozen in familiar remoteness—
they were then, and are closer now, as
they melt and rush into the spill-
ways: "one critical axis of the crystal
structure of ice remains dominant after
the melt"—believe that?

                or live there, they would say in
                the shade I am now competent
                for, the shell still furled but
                some nuclear stream

                        melted from it.
                                The air plays
                on its crown, the
                                prince of life
                                        or its
                        patent, its
                        price. The absent
                        sun (on the
        trees of the field) now does strike
                        so gently
        on the whitened and uneven ice
                        sweet day so calm
        the glitter is the war now released,
        I hear the guns for the first time

Or maybe think so; the eloquence of melt
is however upon me, the path become a
stream, and I lay that down
trusting the ice to withstand the heat; with
that warmth / ah some modest & gentle
       competence a man could live
       with so little
             more.

Price Tag Song

OK and relevant to the
    cosmos, scarce of
              air said
aunt Theoria, the scar
    city is not for
    resale or photograph
             ic repro
    duct
          ion I mean at
least you can't look all
         the time out
    of sight or mind the
            choice is
sheer care
    less debauchery I count, as
    three two one &
          scarce
the part healed city
         where we start
         led in
            sects live

The Common Gain, Reverted

The street is a void in the sequence of man,
as he sleeps by its side, in rows that house
his dreams. Where he lives, which is the
light from windows, all the Victorian grandeur
of steam from a kitchen range. The street
is a void, its surface slips, shines and is
marked with nameless thoughts. If we could
level down into the street! Run across by
the morning traffic, spread like shadows, the
commingling of thoughts with the defeat we
cannot love

                Those who walk heavily
                carry their needs, or lack
                of them, by keeping their
                eyes directed at the ground
                before their feet. They are

said to trudge when in fact their empty thoughts
unroll like a crimson carpet before their
gentle & delicate pace. In any street the pattern
of inheritance is laid down, the truth is for our
time in cats-eyes, white markings, gravel
left from the last fall of snow. We proceed
down it in dreams, from house to house which
spill nothing on to the track, only light on the
edge of the garden. The way is of course speech
and a tectonic emplacement, as gradient it
moves easily, like a void

                It is now at this
                time the one presence
                of fact, our maze
                through which we

                         tread the shadow or
                         at mid-day pace
level beneath our own. And in whichever form
we are possessed the surface is sleep again and
we should be thankful. By whatever movement,
I share the anonymous gift, the connivance
in where to go as what I now find myself
to have in the hand. The nomad is perfect
but the pure motion which has no track is
utterly lost; even the Esquimaux look for sled
markings, though on meeting they may not speak.
                         The street that is the
                         sequence of man
                         is the light of his
                         most familiar need,
to love without being stopped for some im-
mediate bargain, to be warm and tired
without some impossible flame in the heart.
As I walked up the hill this evening and felt
the rise bend up gently against me I knew
that the void was gripped with concentration.
Not mine indeed but the sequence of fact,
the lives spread out, it is a very wild and
distant resort that keeps a man, wandering
at night, more or less in his place.

Aristeas, in Seven Years

Gathering the heat to himself, in one thermic
hazard, he took himself out: to catch up with
the tree, the river, the forms of alien vantage
I *and hence the first way*
> by theft into the upper world—"a
> natural development from the mixed
> economy in the drier or bleaker
> regions, where more movement was
> necessary"—and thus the
floodloam, the deposit, borrowed for
the removal. Call it inland, his
nose filled with steam & his brief cries.
Aristeas took up it
> seems with the
singular as the larch
> tree, the
> Greek sufficient
for that. From Marmora

And sprang with that double twist into the
middle world and thence took flight over the
Scythian hordes and to the Hyperborean,
touch of the north wind
> carrying with him Apollo. Song
> his transport but this divine
> insistence the *pastural clan*:
sheep, elk, the wild deer. In each case
the presence in embryo, god of the shep-
herd and fixed in the movement of flock.
Wrung over the real tracts. If he was
frozen like the felted eagle of Pazyryk,

he too had the impossible lower twist,
the spring into the middle, the air.
> From here comes
> the north wind, the
> remote animal
> gold—how did
>> he, do we, know
>> or trust, this?
> Following the raven and
> sniffing hemp as the
> *other* air, it was
himself as the singular that he knew and
could outlast in the long walk by the
underground sea. Where he was as
> the singular
> location so completely portable
> that with the merest black
> wings he could survey the
> stones and rills in their
> complete mountain courses,
2 *in name the displacement*
> Scythic.
And his songs were invocations in no frenzy
of spirit, but clear and spirituous tones from the
pure base of his mind; he heard the small
currents in the air & they were truly his aid.
In breath he could speak out into the northern
air and the phrasing curved from his mouth
and nose, into the cold mountain levels. It
was the professed Apollo, free of the festive line,
> powdered with light snow.

And looking down, then, it is no outlay
> to be seen in

the forests, or
scattered rising
of ground. No
        cheap cigarettes nothing
        with the god in this
        climate is free of duty
moss, wormwood as the cold
star, the dwarf Siberian pine
as from the morainal deposits
of the last deglaciation.
Down there instead the long flowing hair,
of great herds of sheep and cattle, the
drivers of these, their feet more richly
        thickened in use than
        any slant of their
        mongoloid face or
        long, ruched garments.
With his staff, the larch-pole, that again the
singular and one axis of the errant world.

Prior to the pattern of settlement then, which
is the passing flocks fixed into wherever
        they happened to stop,
the spirit demanded the orphic metaphor
3 *as fact*
that they did migrate and the spirit excursion
was no more than the need and will of the
flesh. The term, as has been pointed out,
        is bone, the
        flesh burned or rotted off but the
        branch calcined like what
        it was: like that: as itself
        the skeleton of the possible
        in a heap and covered with

stones or a barrow.
Leaving the flesh vacant then, in a fuller's shop,
Aristeas removed himself for seven years
into the steppes, preparing his skeleton and the
song of his departure, his flesh anyway touched
     by the in-
     vading Cimmerian
     twilight: "ruinous"
     as the old woman's
     prophecy.
          And who he was took the
          collection of seven
          years to thin out, to the
          fume laid across where
     he went, direction north,

4   *no longer settled*
   but settled now into length; he wore that
   as risk. The garment of birds' feathers,
   while he watched the crows fighting the
       owls with the curling tongues
       of flame proper to the Altaic
       hillside, as he was himself
          more than this. The
     spread is more, the
         vantage is singular
     as the clan is without centre.
          Each where as
     the extent of day deter-
         mines, where the
     sky holds (the brightness
         dependent on that).
And Apollo is in any case seasonal, the
divine "used only of a particular god,
never as a general term." The Hyper-

borean paradise was likewise no general
term but the mythic duration of
                spirit into the bone
                laid out in patterns
                on the ground
            "the skulls are sent on hunting
            journeys, the foot-prints alongside;
            that towards which they journey
            they turn them towards, so that
            they will follow behind."
                From the fuller's shop as from
                the camp of the seal hunter,
5   *some part of the bone must be twisted*
    & must twist, as the stages of Cimmerian
    wandering, viz:
                1. 1800–13th Century B.C., north
                of the Caucasus, then
                2. 13th–8th Centuries, invaded
                by the Scythians and deflected
                southwards & to the west. And
                3. after that, once more displaced
                (8th Century to maybe 500 B.C.),
                the invasion of Asia Minor,
    "ruinous", as any settled and complaisant fixture
    on the shoreline would regard the movement of
    pressure irreducible by trade or bribery. Hence
    the need to catch up, as a response to cheap money
                and how all that huddle could
                be drawn out
            into the tenuous upper
                reach, the fine chatter
            of small birds under the
                head of the sky
            (sub divo columine)

on the western slope of the Urals and the scatter
of lightning, now out of doors & into
      the eagle span,
6 *the true condition of bone*
which is no more singular or settled or the
entitled guardian even, but the land of the
dead. Why are they lost, why do they
      always wander, as if seeking
      their end and drawing after them
      the trail and fume of burning hemp?
      Or they are not lost but
      passing: "If thoughtless abandonment
      to the moment were really a blessing, I
      had actually been in 'the Land of the
      Blessed'."
But it was not blessing, rather a fact so
hard-won that only the twist in middle
air would do it anyway, so even he be wise
or with any recourse to the darkness of
his tent. The sequence of issue is no
      more than this,
      Apollo's price, staff
      leaning into the
      ground and out
      through the smoke-hole.
    It is the spirit which dies
    as the figure of change, which
    is the myth and fact of extent,
    which thus does start from
    Marmora, or Aklavik, right
      out of the air.
    No one harms these people: they
      are sacred and have no
    weapons. They sit or pass, in

the form of divine song,
they are free in the apt form of
        displacement. They change
their shape, being of the essence as
        a figure of extent. Which
for the power in rhyme
7   *is gold, in this northern clime*
which the Greeks so held to themselves and
        which in the steppe was no more
        than the royal figment.
                This movement was of
        course cruel beyond belief, as this
        was the risk Aristeas took
with him. The conquests were for the motive of
sway, involving massive slaughter as the
obverse politics of claim. That is, slaves and
animals, *life* and not value: "the western Sar-
matian tribes lived side by side not in a loose
tribal configuration, but had been welded
        into an organised imperium
        under the leadership of one
        royal tribe." Royalty
as *plural*. Hence the calendar as taking of
life, which left gold as the side-issue, pure
        figure.

Guarded by the griffins, which lived close to the
mines, the gold reposed as the divine brilliance,
petrology of the sea air, so far from the shore.
        The beasts dug the metal out with
        their eagle beaks, rending in the
        cruel frost of that earth, and
yet they were the guardians, the figure of flight
and heat and the northern twist of the axis.

His name Aristeas, absent for
these seven years: we should
pay them or steal, it is no
more than the question they ask.

REFERENCES

A.P. Vaskovskiy, "A Brief Outline of the Vegetation, Climate, and Chronology of the Quaternary Period in the Upper Reaches of the Kolyma and Indigirka Rivers and on the Northern Coast of the Sea of Okhotsk" (1959), in H.N. Michael (ed.), *The Archaeology and Geomorphology of Northern Asia: Selected Works* (Arctic Institute of North America, Anthropology of the North: Translations from Russian Sources, 5; Toronto, 1964)

J. Harmatta, *Studies on the History of the Sarmatians* (Magyar-Görög Tanulmányok, 30; Budapest, 1950)

Herodotus, *History*, 4; Longinus, *On the Sublime*, 10

T. Sulimirski, "The Cimmerian Problem," *Bulletin of the Institute of Archaeology* (University of London), 2 (1959), 45–64

G.S. Hopkins, "Indo-European *Deiwos* and Related Words," *Language Dissertations Published by the Linguistic Society of America* (Supplement to *Language*), XII (1932)

K. Rasmussen, *The Netsilik Eskimos; Social Life and Spiritual Culture* (Report of the Fifth Thule Expedition, 1921–24, Vol. VIII, Nos. 1–2; Copenhagen, 1931)

E.D. Phillips, "The Legend of Aristeas: Fact and Fancy in Early Greek Notions of East Russia, Siberia, and Inner Asia," *Artibus Asiae*, XVIII, 2 (1955), 161–177

E.D. Phillips, "A Further Note on Aristeas," *Artibus Asiae*, XX, 2–3 (1957), 159–162

J. Partanen, "A Description of Buriat Shamanism," *Journal de la Société Finno-Ougrienne*, LI (1941–42), 1–34

H.N. Michael (ed.), *Studies in Siberian Shamanism* (Arctic Institute of North America, Anthropology of the North: Translations from Russian Sources, 4; Toronto, 1963), especially the two papers by A.F. Anisimov: "The Shaman's Tent of the Evenks and the Origin of the Shamanistic Rite" (1952) and "Cosmological Concepts of the Peoples of the North" (1959)

J. Duchemin, *La Houlette et la Lyre: Recherche sur les Origines Pastorales de la Poésie*, Vol. 1: *Hermès et Apollon* (Paris, 1960)

M.S. Ipşiroğlu, *Malerei der Mongolen* (München, 1965)

Señor Vázquez Speaking and Further Soft Music to Eat By

So today it is quite hot again and the
erotic throb of mere air replaces the traffic;
we (the warmed-up) are not separate
from the body flowing into and just being
with air. So delectable, another sense for
presence, glandular pressure; so all
       the dark air comes running
       up like some woven thing,
       soft like our own possessions.
We read about that in cheap paperbacks—maybe
today it's the turn of the scarlet athlete.
Anyway, the angelic hosts were undisturbed
in their eminence of domain, not caring
at all for charter or land reform. In that
sense mostly far distant from the Colombian
peasants whose current leader is so
evidently named by a small promethean gesture.
       To return, this is an
       intimately physical place,
       picked out of the air like
forbidden fruit. So much air and so close I
can feel the lunar caustic I once used in
a lab note-book headed "analysis". Now
it's Laforgue again, the evening a deep city
of velvet and the Parisian nitrates washed off
into the gutters with the storm-water. In the
more entire flarings of sheet lightning the
rain-drops glittered violently in their
descent, like a dream of snake's eyes.

All this the static and
final saturation of air:
the physical world in
which, somewhere out in the Andes or in
the jungle valleys the same bitter spasm
is fought, for life and traffic: it is the
air, we breathe and if
now it
trembles like some satiric
sexual excitement we
are no more than the air we
now are, baffled. The angels have
no reason to worry, about that.

Thoughts on the Esterházy
Court Uniform

I walk on up the hill, in the warm
sun and we do not return, the place is
entirely musical. No person can live there
& what is similar is the deeper resource, the
now hidden purpose. I refer directly to my
own need, since to advance in the now fresh &
sprouting world must take on some musical
sense. Literally, the grace & hesitation of
modal descent, the rhyme unbearable, the
coming down through the prepared delay and
once again we are there, beholding the
complete elation of our end.

       Each move
into the home world is that same loss; we
do mimic the return and the pulse very
slightly quickens, as our motives flare in
the warm hearth. What I have is then already
lost, is so much there I can only come down
to it again, my life slips into music &
increasingly I cannot take much more of this.
The end cadence deferred like breathing, the
birthplace of the poet: all put out their lights
and take their instruments away with them.

How can we sustain such constant loss.
I ask myself this, knowing that the world
is my pretext for this return through it, and
that we go more slowly as we come back
more often to the feeling that rejoins the whole.
Soon one would live in a sovereign point and

still we don't return, not really, we look back
and our motives have more courage in
structure than in what we take them to be.
The sun makes it easier & worse, like the
music late in the evening, but should it start
to rain—the world converges on the idea
of return. To our unspeakable loss; we make
sacred what we cannot see without coming
back to where we were.

           Again is the sacred
word, the profane sequence suddenly graced, by
coming back. More & more as we go deeper
I realise this aspect of hope, in the sense of
the future cashed in, the letter returned to sender.
How can I straighten the sure fact that
we do *not* do it, as we regret, trust, look
forward to, etc? Since each time what
we have is increasingly the recall, not
the subject to which we come. Our chief
loss is ourselves; that's where I am, the
sacral link in a profane world, we each do
this by the pantheon of hallowed times.
Our music the past tense:

                    if it would only
level out into some complete migration of
sound. I could then leave unnoticed, bring nothing
with me, allow the world free of its displace-
ment. Then I myself would be the
complete stranger, not watching jealously
over names. And yet home is easily our
idea of it, the music of decent and proper
order, it's this we must leave in some quite
specific place if we are not to carry it
everywhere with us.

I know I will go back
down & that it will not be the same though
I shall be sure it is so. And I shall be even
deeper by rhyme and cadence, more held
to what isn't mine. Music is truly
the sound of our time, since it is how we most
deeply recognise the home we may not
have: the loss is trust and you could
reverse that without change.
                                          With such
patience maybe we can listen to the rain
without always thinking about rain, we
trifle with rhyme and again is the
sound of immortality. We think we have
it & we must, for the sacred resides in this;
once more falling into the hour of my birth, going
down the hill and then in at the back door.

A Sonnet to Famous Hopes

Then the mind fills with snow the
free, open syllables of reward. All the
limbs respond, to this my eyes see, there
the sense of an immense patch—the north
atlantic wake. A line of scrubby trees, those
fields still not ready but the snow, is still
the physical rain. Also hopeless, as if dead
with strain and every nerve, in the dismal
cathedral a grey waste. But the freedom plant
springs alert, in its curious way and reserved
in guesswork, now in biblical sequence. O
Jerusalem you are no less than this, Cairo
and Massachusetts, trust your eyes only
when they fill with more than, the price of
what you see. As what I feel about it &
meanwhile, the retinal muscle is bound to
another world, the banks of snow are
immense. The patch of salvation, so we are
too late not paranoid or jewish yet but
the snow fills, me with reward & with me, the
road is the tariff: above all then great
banks of cloud tether my elate muscle, to
nothing less & its fields—still fresh & green.

Whose Dust Did You Say

How old how far & how much the
years tear at us the shreds of cloth as
I think of them and the great palaces
with courts & the sounds of mirth
merriment in the darkness within the
great dream of the night. I live still
with the bitter habits of that fire &
disdain I live in it surrounded by
little else who can impair or bound
that empire of destined habitation
or go off into that coyly drab town
by slow stages or by any other damn
thing else who can who would waste
his time who would fritter his time
away how the years now do encircle
the season and when is a wage a
salary by dead reckoning from the
merest centre of the earth the
mere & lovely centre, of the earth.

A Dream of Retained Colour

We take up with the black branch
in the street, it is our support and
control, what we do with life in
the phase now running on. From here
each time the glitter does settle out,
around some lamp, some fried-up
commercial scene we live in
support of and for. Who is this
that may just do the expected
thing; not the magic silence
of the inward eye you may be quite
positive. TV beams romantically into
the biosphere, plant food is our
daily misery. Mine: light & easy,
the victim-path is so absurd.

Misery is that support & control: the
force of sympathy is a claim no one
can pay for. We are indeed supplanted
and I know the light is all bribery,
daylight, electric, the matching stroke.

Uncertain whether the stars of my
inner canopy are part of this
brittle crust I watch them often.
The moon is still silent, I count that
a favour unpurchased, but the
scintillant clusters are the true test:

how much then *are*
we run, managed by
the biograph & pre-
dictive incision, it
must be possible to set the question
up & have it operational, in time
to restore the eye of fate: Lucifer, with-
out any street lamps or TV. The
branch is rained on, it does nothing,
the event is unresponsive / & attending
to such infantile purchase is the
murderous daily income of sympathy.

The stars then being
ideas without win-
dows, *what* should we
do by watching, is
it true: is it true? Starlight is the
new torture, seraphic host, punishment
of the visionary excess. What else, they
glide with their income intact, how often
they travel. What they do in this
social favour, that and how with, is
it true. The prism
of mere life is un-
bearable, plants and
animals in their
sæcular changes, eaten up with will-power.
Who would believe in the victim, as, in
such general diversion, who would need to.
O you who drive past in my dream-car

of the century, lead me by no still waters,
don't touch me with the needle. I'm watch-
ing no one, the torture is immaculate and
conserved, I'd love to go so much it
> isn't true it
> really isn't true.

3 Sentimental Tales

one

further towards the
sky now well don't
be such a damn
nuisance you'll break
the cord what of
that it's nearly time
for supper we must
eat the clouds range
in their places the
tide's up the other
waits for him

two

that's wormwood we'll
pick some we'll
hang it up the line
holds back a tidal
point eastwards it's
nice there anyway
why take the
trouble the lines
dip lean & famous

three

you could say it
was the water the
birds often come
here a nice glide
before dark I
must say the
salt thickens mere
prospects and any
way they could hardly
get better now
could they as
the wind freshens they
do so slowly

Foot and Mouth

Every little shift towards comfort is a manoeuvre
of capital loaned off into the jungle of interest: see
how the banks celebrate their private season, with
brilliant swaps across the Atlantic trapeze. Such del-
icate abandon: we hold ourselves comfortingly braced
beneath, a safety-net of several millions & in what
we shall here call north Essex the trend is certainly
towards ease, time off to review those delicious values
traced in frost on the window or which wage-labour
used to force to the Friday market. Actually as I look
out the silly snow is collapsing into its dirty self
again, though I don't feel the cold as I have thought-
fully taped out the draughts with Pressure Sensitive
Tape (also known as RUBAN ADHESIF and NASTRO AD-
HESIVO). Thus my own sphere of interest, based on
a quite sharp fahrenheit differential, contains no trace
of antique posture; I'm waiting for the soup to boil
and even the slow, pure, infinitely protracted recall
of a train-ride in northern Ontario (the Essex of north
America) can't fully divert me from the near prospect
of Campbell's Cream of Tomato Soup, made I see at
King's Lynn, Norfolk. Another fine local craft, you
don't need to believe all you read about the New York
art industry: "the transfer of capitalistic production
to the foreign market frees the latter completely from
the limitations imposed by its own consumer capacity."
And note that *completely* here, as I do while looking at
this dirty cold patch of road and suchlike, thinking
of cree indians and their high-bevelled cheeks &
almost ready for my skilfully seasoned 10½ oz. treat.

No one in Minnesota would believe, surely, that the dollar
could *still* be whipping up tension about this? I am
assured by this thought and by the freedom it brings,
& by the garishly French gold medal won by my soup in 1900.

Star Damage at Home

The draft runs deeper now & the motion
relaxes its hold, so that I pass freely from
habit to form and to the sign complete
without unfolding—the bright shoots in the
night sky or the quick local tremor of leaves.
Where this goes is a scattered circle, each
house set on a level and related by time
to the persons whose lives now openly
have them in train. Each one drawn in
by promise recalled, just as the day itself
unlocks the white stone. Rain as it
falls down turns to the level of name, the
table slanting off with its concealed glint.
And what is the chance for survival, in this
fertile calm, that we could mean what
we say, and hold to it? That some star
not included in the middle heavens should
pine in earth, not shine above the skies and
those cloudy vapours? That it really should
burn with fierce heat, explode its fierce &
unbearable song, blacken the calm it comes
near. A song like a glowing rivet strikes
out of the circle, we must make room for
the celestial victim; it is amongst us and
fallen with hissing fury into the ground. Too
lovely the ground and my confidence as I
walk so evenly above it: we must mean the
entire force of what we shall come to say.
I cannot run with these deeply implicit
motions, the person is nothing, there should be
torture in our midst. Some coarsely exploited

money-making trick, fast & destructive, shrill
havoc to the murmur of names. The
blaze of violent purpose at least, struck
through : light : we desire what we mean
& we must mean that & consume to
ash any simple deflection:

    I will not be led
    by the mean-
    ing of my
    tinsel past or
    this fecund hint

I merely live in. Destruction is too
good for it, like Cassius I flaunt the path
of some cosmic disaster. Fix the eye on
the feast of hatred forcing the civil war
in the U.S., the smoke towering above the
mere words splitting like glass into the
air. The divinity of light spread through
the day, the mortal cloud like no more than
heat haze, that thing is the idea of blood
raised to a final snow-capped abstraction. I
mean what the name has in its charge,
being not deceived by the dispersal which
sets it down. We live in compulsion, no
less, we must have the damage by which
the stars burn in their courses, we take/
set/twist/dispose of the rest. There is
no pause, no mild admixture. This is to
crush it to the centre, the angelic song shines
with embittered passion; there is no price
too high for the force running uncontrolled
into the cloud nearest the earth. We live here
and must mean it, the last person we are.

One Way at Any Time

Through the steamed-up windows it says
"Thermal Insulation Products" I can't see
where it's come from, as the warm steamy
sound puffs out from the jukebox. The girl
leans over to clear off my plate, hey I've not
finished yet, the man opposite without think-
ing says must be on piecework and his
regular false teeth gleam like sardines. But
the twist here is that it's all in that yokel
talk they have for the rustics and this man
is in overalls, his boy about nine silent
beside him. The driver opposite looks as
if from some official car, he carries unworn
black leather gloves & wears a black cap,
with a plastic vizor. He has a watch-
chain across his waistcoat and a very
metallic watch on his wrist—he is not
functional in anything but the obvious
way but how will he too speak? Mc-
Cormick International rumbles past
in truly common dialect, diesel in low
gear but the boy is still quiet. His teeth are
the real thing, crooked incisors as he
bites into B & B his father's mate sways
with natural endorsement back and forward
in his chair left by six he says and I don't
know whether a.m. or p.m. The girl shouts
and the young driver in uniform gives
an urban, movie-style flick of a nod as
he pushes back his chair it is Bristol it

is raining I wish I were Greek and could
trust all I hear but suppose anyway
that one of them turned out to be Irish?

Acquisition of Love

The children rise and fall as they
watch, they burn in the sun's coronal
display, each child is the fringe
and he advances at just that blinding
gradient. As I try to mend the broken
mower, its ratchet jammed somewhere
inside the crank-case, I feel the
blood all rush in a separate spiral,
each genetically confirmed in the
young heartlands beyond. The curious
ones have their courses set towards
fear and collapse, faces switch on and
off, it is not any image of learning
but the gene pool itself defines these
lively feelings. I get the casing off,
sitting on the flat stone slab by the
front door, you would think fortunes
could be born here and you would
be wrong. Their childish assertion is
bleeding into the centre, we are determined
that they shall do this; they look outwards
to our idea of the planet. Their blood
is battered by this idea, the rules for
the replication of pattern guide their dreams
safely into our dreams. The two ratchets
are both rusted in; I file out their
slots and brush out the corroded
flakes with oil. They watch, and
what they watch has nothing to do
with anything. What they do is an
inherited print, I lend it to them

just by looking & only their blood
seems to hold out against the complete
neuro-chemical entail. I guess their
capacity in pints, the dream-like membranes
which keep their faces ready to see. The
mower works now, related to nothing
but the hand and purpose, the fear of
collapse is pumped round by each linked
system & the borrowed warmth of the heart.

Questions for the Time Being

All right then *no* stoic composure as the
self-styled masters of language queue up to
apply for their permits. That they own and
control the means of production (or at least
the monopoly of its more dangerous aspects)
seems not to have struck home. But it
must, or hysterical boredom will result and
we shall all think that creative paranoia
has now finally reached these shores—and as
if we didn't invent it anyway, as Wyndham
Lewis tried so fiercely to explain. And in the
face of the "new frankness" in immaculate
display in the highest places, why should
the direct question not be put: if any discrete
class with an envisaged part in the social process
is not creating its own history, then who is doing
it for them? Namely, what is anyone waiting
for, either resigned or nervous or frantic from
time to time? Various forms dodge through
the margins of a livelihood, but so much talk
about the underground is silly when it would re-
quire a constant effort to keep below the surface,
when almost everything is exactly that, the
mirror of a would-be alien who won't see how
much he is at home. In consequence also the
idea of change is briskly seasonal, it's too cold
& thus the scout-camp idea of revolution stands
in temporary composure, waiting for spring. All
forms of delay help this farce, that our restrictions
are temporary & that the noble fiction is to have
a few good moments, which represent what we know

ought to be ours. Ought to be, that makes me
wince with facetiousness: we/you/they, all the
pronouns by now know how to make a sentence
work with *ought to*, and the stoic at least saves
himself that extremity of false vigilance.

Yet living in hope is so silly when our desires
are so separate, not part of any mode or con-
dition except language & there they rest on
the false mantelpiece, like ornaments of style.
And expectancy is equally silly when what we think
of is delay, or gangsterism of the moment, some
Micawberish fantasy that we can snatch the controls
when the really crucial moment turns up. Not with-
out asbestos gloves we can't, the wheel is permanently
red-hot, no one on a new course sits back and
switches on the automatic pilot. Revisionist plots
are everywhere and our pronouns haven't even
drawn up plans for the first coup. Really it's
laughable & folks talk of discontent or waiting
to see what they can make of it. How much
cash in simple gross terms went through the
merger banks in the last three months? Buy one
another or die; but the cultured élite, our squad
of pronouns with their lingual backs to the wall,
prefer to keep everything in the family. The up-
shot is simple & as follows: 1. No one has any right
to mere idle discontent, even in conditions of most
extreme privation, since such a state of arrested
insight is actively counter-productive; 2. Con-
tentment or sceptical calm will produce
instant death at the next jolt & intending
suicides should carry a card at least exonerating
the eventual bystanders; 3. What goes on in a

language is the corporate & prolonged action
of worked self-transcendence—other minor verbal
delays have their uses but the scheme of such
motives is at best ambiguous; 4. Luminous
take-off shows through in language forced into any
compact with the historic shift, but in a given con-
dition such as now not even elegance will come
of the temporary nothing in which life goes on.

Starvation / Dream

The fire still glides down
in the hearth, the pale season
and the leaky boat drops
slowly downstream. Like emeralds
the remote figure of a
remote capital gain: the case
of fire rests in a flicker, just
short of silence. So the dream
still curls in its horizon of
total theft, cooled by the misty
involvement of dew, and at once
it is clear, finally, that this
is not our planet: we have come
to the wrong place. We steal
everything we have—why else
are we driven by starved passion
to the dishonour of force? The
Russian trick was to burn up
wads of banknotes, so as to
clear the imperial stain, the hedged
& tree-lined avenues of our desires.
And what we dream we want is
the whole computed sum of plants and
animals of this middle world, the
black lands called up by our
patient & careful visits. By any
ritual of purpose we extend the idea
of loan and we dream of it, the
payment of all our debts. But we
never shall, we have no single gain
apart from the disguise of how far

we say we earn. The ground out-
side mistily involves itself with its
contour, the leaky boat glides down
the morning flood, in this rival
dream all our enemies are with us
and the animals & plants shall
take nourishment from the same
silent and passionless table.

Smaller than the Radius of the Planet

There is a patch like ice in the sky this
evening & the wind tacks about, we are
both stopped/fingered by it. I lay out my
unrest like white lines on the slope, so that
something out of broken sleep will land
there. Look up, a vale of sorrow opened by
eyes anywhere above us, the child spread out
in his memory of darkness. And so, then, the
magnetic influence of Venus sweeps its
shiver into the heart/brain or hypothalamus,
we are still here, I look steadily at nothing.
"The gradient of the decrease may be de-
termined by the spread in intrinsic lumin-
osities"—the ethereal language of love in
brilliant suspense between us and the
hesitant arc. Yet I need it too and keep
one hand in my pocket & one in yours,
waiting for the first snow of the year.

Crown

The hours are taken slowly out of the
city and its upturned faces—a rising fountain
quite slim and unflowering as it
is drawn off. The arrangements of work
swell obscurely round the base of the
Interior Mountain, in the pale house with
its parody of stairs. The air is cold; a
pale sunlight is nothing within the con-
strictions of trust in the throat, in
the market-place. Or the silver police
station, the golden shops, all holy in this
place where the sound of false shouts too
much does reconcile the face and hands.
Yet the feet tread about in the dust, cash slides
& crashes into the registers, the slopes
rise unseen with the week and can still
burn a man up. Each face a purging
of venom, an absent coin, oh why as the
hours pass and are drawn off do the
shoulders break, down to their possessions,
when at moments and for days the city
is achieved as a glance—inwards, across,
the Interior Mountain with its cliffs
pale under frost. And the question rises
like helium in its lightness, not held down
by any hands, followed by the faces dis-
owned by the shoes & overcoat settling in
behind the wheel and pulling the door shut.

Thus the soul's discursive fire
veers with the wind; the love
of any man is turned
by the mere and cunning front:

No hand then but to coin, no
face further than
needs be, the sounds fall
quickly into the gutters:

And from this the waters thin into their
ascendent vapour, the pillar of cloud; it
stands over the afternoon already half-
dark. No one is fearful, I see them all
stop to look into the sky and my famished
avowals cast the final petals. It is the
Arabian flower of the century, the question
returned upon itself; the action of month and
hour is warm with cinnamon & clear water,
the first slopes rise gently at our feet.

Love

Noble in the sound which
marks the pale ease
of their dreams, they ride
the bel canto of our
time: the patient en-
circlement of Narcissus &
as he pines I too
am wan with fever,
have fears which set
the vanished child above
reproach. Cry as you
will, take what you
need, the night is young
and limitless our greed.

Night Song

The white rose trembles by the step   it is
uncalled for in the fading daylight and
tiny plants sprout from between the stones

Soon Mizar will take the tawny sky
into protection   they will soon be calling
for the sick ones and all our passing

sounds will rise into the horn and be
cast outwards   scattered   the scale rises
like a tide and the frail craft is afloat

Who would believe it   yet the waters are
rough and the seabirds fly unblinking as
if wind were the ointment they wished for

Come back to the step I call as the house
turns and it is almost night   but there is
no end to the peace claimed by the sick

body and no relief for the mere lack of
fever by which now I lean from the step
and touch at the bare twigs with my wrist

A Stone Called Nothing

Match the stone, the milk running in the
middle sea, take your way with them. The way
is the course as you speak, gentle chatter:
the lights dip as the driver presses the
starter & the bus pulls away to leave
for the moonstruck fields of the lower paid.
Gentle chatter, match the stone, we are
running into the sea. Pay your fare, have
the road beamed out:

                nay, eat as much
bread as you find, and leave the wide earth
to pursue its way; go to the brink of the
river, and drink as much as you need, and
pass on, and seek not to know whence
it comes, or how it flows.

                    A good course
in the middle sea, we swing into a
long rising bend. The equinox is our line for
the present, who is to love that: the thought
dries off into the arch ready for it. Faintest
of stellar objects, I defy you and yet this
devastation curls on, out over the road. Are
we so in the black frost, is this what we pay
for as the ruined names fade into Wilkes Land,
its "purity of heart"?

                  Do your best to have your
foot cured, or the disease of your eye, that you
may see the light of the sun, but do not enquire
how much light the sun has, or how high it
rises.

The devastation is aimless; folded with-
out recompense, change down to third do any
scandalous thing, the gutters run with milk.
The child of any house by the way is something
to love, I devise that as an appeal to Vulcan, to
open the pit we cannot fall into. Failure
without falling, the air is a frozen passage,
the way bleached out, we are silent now. The
child is the merest bent stick; I cannot move.
There should be tongues of fire & yet now
the wipers are going, at once a thin rain is
sucked into the glass, oh I'll trust anything.

The babe, when it comes to its mother's breast,
takes the milk and thrives, it does not search
for the root and well-spring from which it
flows so. It sucks the milk and empties
the whole measure
                              : listen to the sound yet
we go on moving, the air is dry, I seem
to hear nothing. It is for the time an aimless
purchase, where are we now you say I
think or not /go on/get off/quiet/ match the stone.

John in the Blooded Phoenix

Days are uncertain now and move by
flux gradients laid by the rare min-
erals, sodium in dreams of all the body
drawn into one transcendent muscle:
the dark shopfront at 3 a.m. But
we are close to the ancient summits
of a figure cast for the age, the gas-
fire we sit by, the sharp smell of burning
orange-peel. The axis of landform runs
through each muted interchange, the
tilt is a plausible deflexion of energy / now
we are not at the side of anything.
In the vision made by memories of metal
we walk freely as if by omen over an
open terrace, of land like chalky
sediment in soft water. It is the gas-fire
that does it, I despise nothing which
comes near a skyline as old as this.
We could pace in our own fluids, we speak
in celestial parlance, our chemistry is
reduced to transfusion. Who would for-
bid fair Cleopatra smiling / on his poor
soul, for her sweet sake still dying? If
he were he is, the condition of prompt
dilatancy is exactly this: the palest
single spark in all the Pleiades.

Chemins de Fer

It is a forest of young pines and now we
are eating snow in handfuls, looking at the
towers which when the light topsoil is warm
again will carry the firewatchers. From here there
is no simple question of *preparing to leave* or
making our way. Even the thinnest breath of
wind wraps round the intense lassitude, that
an undeniably political centre keeps watch; the
switch of light and shadow is packed with
foreign tongues. I shall not know my own
conjecture. The plants stare at my ankles in
stiffness, they carry names I cannot recognise.

> Yet in the air, still
> now, I am claimed
> by the memory of
> how the join, the
> incessant *lapping*, is
> already reported in

talk to a human figure. Again he is
watchful, the dream slides right up to the
true Adam and he keeps silent among the
branches. The approach, here, of streamy recall
seems like the touch of Europe, an invert logic
brought in with too vivid a pastoral sense,
too certain for Alsace, the double eagle or the
Gulf of Lions. He is a dark outline, already

> struck by sacred
> emptiness. He goes
> slowly, her body
> fades into reason,

   the memory ever-
   green and planted,
   like the lost child.
And so slowly, still, draining gradually into
the Rhine, the huge barges freeze in the heat
of trade. How much power, the machine gun in
a Polish scenario, black and white fade into those
passionless excursions of childhood. The small
copse, water rusted in, an adventure! With which
the flimsy self pivots in wilful envy and lusts
after its strange body, its limbs gorged & inert.

As It Were an Attendant

Proceeding still in the westward face, and like
a life underwater: that facade
                                   sheer and abrupt,
the face in all that shot towards venus, march
on the pentagon, all the prodigious cycle of ages.
Going on then any person still frequent, fixed by
the sun in that euclidean concept of "day", takes
a pause and at once is the face
                                   or some account
of it: *mostly* we are so rushed. Harassment is
not on the switch, playback of the perfect
                                             darling
and late again—we can begin with the warmup
about the politics of melody / that one, and
please you say at once, not *again*.
                                   By the face
we converse about stars, starlight & their twinkle,
since sweetly it subsides and by proceeding,
a long file above water, single
            laced after this
            jabber we keep it
            all going, at one time
            it is just that,
                        gone; the
                        rest is some
                        pale & cheshire
                        face. Conspicuous
            by its rays & terrible and grand this
                        is not our feeling
            as blindly I tread to find myself

out of it, running
on before them, accompanying them and
going with them,
there, as I have not known for months,
standing by a hedge: "I
love the shipwrecked man who was betrayed
by misfortune." As a cork rammed in the
century's neck, I see at once the faces who have
unsuccessfully dogged my path—the procession
headed by the old woman who walks & does other
things
maybe she
sings, this is
her song:
Blackie, she
calls (her cat free
of sparks), she
treads with her
face, the grave
carried away

she has stringy hair
water flows at her feet
it is often dark there
nor quick nor neat nor
any thing / along the path leading
up to the Congregational Chapel at
Linton the sepulchral urns mourn
their loss of protein & like its
beautifully fishy stare the frontage
outfaces the morning, the star at evening, like
milk. *Mostly* this is the
end of it, through into some-
thing else, as, statement:

                    the child is so quiet now
                    he has stopped screaming
                    the scarlet drains from
                    his cheeks he is pale and
                    beautiful he will soon be
                    asleep I hope he will
                    not thus too quickly die
in the sky the face Blackie she calls
him & he is there & without passion.

The Corn Burned by Syrius

Leave it with the slender distraction, again this
is the city shaken down to its weakness. Washed-out
green so close to virtue in the early morning,
than which for the curving round to home this
is the fervent companion. The raised bank by
the river, maximum veritas, now we have no
other thing. A small red disc quivers in the street,
we watch our conscious needs swing into this point
and vanish; that it is more cannot be found, no
feature, where else could we go. The distraction
is almost empty, taken up with nothing; if the two
notes sounded together could possess themselves, be
ready in their own maximum: "O how farre
art thou gone from thy Country, not being
driven away, but wandring of thine owne accord."
On the bank an increase of sounds, and walk through
the sky the grass, that any motion is the first
settlement. We plant and put down cryptic slopes
to the damp grass, this passion fading off to the
intensely beaten path: that it should be possessed
of need & desire coiled into the sky, and then dis-
membered into the prairie twitching with herbs,
pale, that it is the city run out and retained
for the thousands of miles allowed, claimed to be so.

Day Light Songs
(1968)

Inhale   breathe deeply and
      there the mountain
        is there are
      flowers streams flow
simple bright goods clutter
        the ravines the
air is thin & heady
      the mountain
respires, is equal to
      the whole

So much, is just
      by pulse then
    the sky clears, again
love is a term
      of shadow and
    the shade flickers
      here, too

Since otherwise snap &
             a false a hope
less polythene lung
        when so easily the
             town fits to
             the stride, we look
at pots of jam we
             look upward

And so when it does
             rain & will glide
down our necks like
             glances into
             the soul, drop
        lets work their
way forward the sinus
        is truly the scent
of the earth, upraised

Who shall make the
          sigh, of the
     waters, sign of
rain & coming down
          over the ridge
the entire air a nod
          to for
     tune, who else

The leaves make drops, drop
          down the great
tent of falling, the
          twigs are inside
     us, we the
branches beyond which
          by which through which
     ever the
          entire brightness ex
          tends

Do not deny this halo
          the shouts are
against nothing we all
          stand at variance
we walk slowly if it
          hurts we rant it
is not less than true oh
          love I tell you so

As now, a term less than
          misty forewarnings
less ready in simple
     motions of cloud
          we breathe the
same motions of habit
     some part of the sky
is constant, that old
          tune, Sonny Boy

Foot, how you press
          me to keep that
     old contact alive
the repeated daily sentiment
          of pace so
     grim, always that
untrusting silence

And the hill is a
          figure, dust in the
     throat
          did you say that
     or was
          it merely spoken
     as love a thirst for
this and both together the
          morning

The whole cloud is bright
     & assembled now
we are drawn by simple
       plea, over
    the membrane and its
      folded parts
into the point, and touch the
     air streaming away

A Note on Metal

(1968)

The early Bronze Age would, I suppose, locate the beginnings of Western alchemy, the theory of quality as *essential*. The emergence of metal technologies (smelting & beating, followed by knowledge of alloys) was clearly a new way with the magical forms through which property resided in substance. Until this stage, weight was the most specific carrier for the inherence of power, and weight was and is a mixed condition, related locally to exertion. The focus of this condition is typically stone; and though this seems most obviously to insist on the compact outer surface, in fact it provides the most important practical & cultic *inside*: the cave. The privilege of that ambiguity about surface gives the painted rock-shelter and the megalithic chamber-tomb the power of formal change, and in this way substance can be extended, by incorporation, to allow the magical and political/social presences their due place.

Whereas with copper, tin (and perhaps antimony), weight coincides with other possible conditions which are less mixed and specific: brightness, hardness, ductility and general ease of working. And further, the abstraction of *property* (characterised as formal rather than substantive) makes the production of alloys a question of technique in the most theoretical sense.[1] Bronze may have been known to the Sumerians at a very early stage, and yet tin is rare in the Near East and must have been imported over considerable distances. The difference between the kinds of intent supporting the movement of bluestones from Pembrokeshire to Wessex, and the Sumerian acquisition of tin from Cornwall or Bohemia, must be obvious.

And through the agency of the most ostensive control of force, namely fire, sword-blades or spear-heads could be forged into a strength infinitely more abstract than the flaking of high-quality flint or the hardening of wooden points. The new quality thus gained was sharp and killed with new speed and power, from a long range. Animal hides could be sewn up with metal bodkins and fish taken with fine wire hooks; the metal ploughshare could cut deeper into the soil and with less effort.[2] The new quality of spiritual transfer was concentrated in these most durable forms of leading edge, seen especially in the flattened motive of ornament, and the history of substance (stone) shifts with complex social implication into the theory of power (metal).

That's a deliberately simplified sketch, because it may well be that this theorising of quality, with its control over weaponry and tillage and hence over life, induced a deeper cultural adherence to substance as the zone of being in which the condition was also limit: the interior knowledge of dying. By death I mean here in particular those forms of life and ritual, the extension of body, in which persistence through material transmutation was an ego-term (even when socialised) rather than one concerned chiefly with the outer world (enemies or animals hunted for food, flesh as object). So that stone becomes the power-substance marking the incorporated extensions of dying, and is still so as a headstone is the vulgar or common correlative of a hope for the after-life.

And in parallel with this reactive development (maybe, an exilic theory of substance) comes the rapid advance of metallurgy, shifting from the transfer of life as power (hunting) into the more settled expectation of reaping what you have already sown; this itself produces the idea of *place* as the chief local fact, which makes mining and the whole extractive industry possible from then on. The threshing of millet or barley must bring a 'purer' and more abstract theory of value; the mixed relativism of substance leads, by varied but in outline predictable stages, to value as a specialised function and hence as dependent on the rate of exchange. The Sumerian settlement was founded on the innovations of metallurgy, and these abstractions of substance were in turn the basis for a politics of *wealth*: the concentration of theoretic power by iconic displacement of substance. The unit of exchange was still the ingot by weight and not yet coins by number, but we are already in what Childe called a 'money economy' as opposed to a 'natural economy': there is already a code of practice for capital loaned out on interest.[3]

For a long time the magical implications of transfer in any shape must have given a muted and perhaps not initially debased sacrality to objects of currency-status, just as fish-hooks and bullets became strongly magical objects in the societies formed around their use. But gradually the item-form becomes iconized, in transitions like that from *aes rude* (irregular bits of bronze), through *aes signatum* (cast ingots or bars) to *aes grave* (the circular stamped coin). The metonymic unit is established, and number replaces strength or power as the chief assertion of presence. In consequence, trade-routes undergo a dramatic expansion, since mercantile theory operates with the most conspicuous success when employed over large inter-cultural distances: "In the Early Bronze Age peninsular Italy, Central Europe, the West Baltic Coastlands, and the British Isles were united by a single system for the distribution of metalware, rooted in the Aegean market."[4]

The clearest instance of this type of change arises probably where a more 'sophisticated' and 'progressive' economy meets an idiom of change and value less efficiently abstracted. The mercantile contact between the sea-borne traders of the Eastern Mediterranean and the peoples of the Anatolian hinterland can show this interaction already by the late Bronze Age (for this region, c. 1600 B.C.). On the great alluvial plains of Asia the condition was one of power rather than value; that is, substance, and not (in the first instance) transfer as exchange. Flocks and herds can be stolen, bartered, given in gift or tribute, so that wealth for the most part is the power of a technique to hold all that, again the politics of limit. Whereas the Greek traders were already middlemen with no political standing, Sardis no city but a commercial centre working on the trick of abstract distance between real supply and real demand. Lydia, as Childe again said, was "a frontier kingdom owing its prosperity to transit trade."[5]

Here finally, and for the first time (according to tradition) arises sheer mercantile distance in the form of *coin*, where the magical resonance of transfer is virtually extinct: "That coined money should have been evolved here [the Eastern Mediterranean] is not surprising, for it was an area of intense commercial activity, encouraged and fostered by natural advantages. The Lydians, 'the first shopkeepers' as Herodotus called them, as well as the neighbouring Ionians, received goods from the caravan routes and river communications across Asia. They had access to safe and sheltered harbours for easy coastwise trade. They exported their famous Chian wines, their purple dye which gave its name to Erythrae, and their Samian pots, but above all they were renowned for their gold, which provided the fabulous wealth of Croesus, and still more fabulous wealth of Midas."[6] And Croesus, the first recorded millionaire, is also the first to devise a bimetallic currency, where even the *theoretic* properties of metal are further displaced, into the stratified functionalism of a monetary system. We are almost completely removed from presence as weight, and at this point the emergence of a complete middle class based on the technique of this removal becomes a real possibility. So that by this stage there *is* the possible contrast of an exilic (left-wing) history of substance.

And yet the shifts are off-set and multiple, and in the earlier stages are accompanied by extensions of awareness newly sharpened by exactly that risk. The literal is *not* magic, for the most part, and it's how the power of displacement side-slipped into some entirely other interest which is difficult, not a simple decision that any one movement is towards ruin. Stone is already the abstraction of standing, of balance; and dying is still the end of a man's self-enrichment, the "reason" why he does it. The North American Indians developed no real metallurgy at all, at any stage of their history.[7] The whole shift and turn is *not* direct (as Childe, too insistently, would have us believe), but rather the increasing speed of displacement which culminates only later in a critical overbalance of intent.[8] If we are confident over the more developed consequences, at the unrecognised turn we are still at a loss to say where or why.

1 Some of the earliest British metal-technologies have been held to include techniques of "smelting, alloying, casting, hammering, grinding and polishing, work in repoussé with punches, traced ornament, perforation with a punch and perhaps also by drilling, riveting, probably the use of a mandrel, and most likely an empirical skill in the exploitation of work-hardening and annealing" (D. Britton, "Traditions of Metal-Working in the Later Neolithic and Early Bronze Age of Britain," *Proceedings of the Prehistoric Society*, N.S. XXIX [1963], p. 279).

2 On the technology of this, see G.E. Fussell, "Ploughs and Ploughing before 1800," *Agricultural History*, XL (1966), 177–186.

3 See also Marc Bloch, "Natural Economy or Money Economy" (1933), in J.E. Anderson (trans.), *Land and Work in Medieval Europe; Selected Papers by Marc Bloch* (London, 1967). Even in the case of early Greek coinage it has been argued that the original intention was not so much in the first place to facilitate trade (external or internal), but rather to establish a system of centralised national wealth which could support a professional military caste; see C.M. Kraay, "Hoards, Small Change and the Origin of Coinage," *Journal of Hellenic Studies*, LXXXIV (1964), 76–91.

4 V.G. Childe, *The Prehistory of European Society* (London, 1962), p. 166.

5 On the overland trade-routes in Asia Minor and traffic in metals (especially copper) see R. Dussaud, "La Lydie et ses voisins aux hautes époques," *Babylonaica*, XI (1930), and in particular the tentative route-map included as plate 1. There is reason to consider this hypothesis of overland trade with the interior as conjectural, but there is little evidence which would refute it. See G.M.A. Hanfmann, "Prehistoric Sardis," in G.E. Mylonas (ed.), *Studies Presented to David Moore Robinson* (Saint Louis, 1951–3), Vol. I, pp. 160–183, and J.M. Birmingham, "The Overland Route across Anatolia in the Eighth and Seventh Centuries B.C.," *Anatolian Studies*, XI (1961), 185–195. On specifically Lydian trade and the monopoly structure of the Lydian mining industry,

see C. Roebuck, *Ionian Trade and Colonization* (New York, 1959), Chap. III and especially note 83 (p. 59) on *kapelos*.

6 A.H. Quiggin, *A Survey of Primitive Money; the Beginnings of Currency* (London, 1949), p. 282. Concerning Midas (briefly) see J.M. Cook, *Greek Settlement in the Eastern Aegean and Asia Minor* (Vol. II, Chap. XXXVIII of the revised *Cambridge Ancient History*, issued in fascicle, Cambridge, 1961), pp. 26–27.

7 Although the almost pure native copper from the Lake Superior region was being hammered into various points, blades and ornaments as early as 2000–1000 B.C. But the forms are in most cases copied directly from earlier types in flint or bone, and none of the smelting or alloy processes was involved. See J.B. Griffin, "Late Quaternary Prehistory in the Northeastern Woodlands," in H.E. Wright Jr., and D.G. Frey (eds.), *The Quaternary of the United States* (Princeton, 1965), p. 663.

8 Urban totalitarianism, for example, as Childe argued in "The Bronze Age," *Past and Present*, 12 (1957), 2–15.

Index of Titles or First Lines